Can cats swim

even if they don't like water?

World Book
answers YOUR questions
- about -
pets and other animals

WORLD BOOK

www.worldbook.com

The questions in this book came from curious kids just like you who want to make sense of the world. They wrote to us at World Book with nothing but a question and a dream that the question they've agonized over would finally be answered.

Some questions made us laugh. Others made us cry. And a few made us question absolutely everything we've ever known. No matter the responses they induced, all the questions were good questions.

There isn't a strict rule for what makes a question good. But asking any question means that you want to learn and to understand. And both of those things are very good.

Adults are always asking, "What did you learn at school today?" Instead, we think they should be asking, **"Did you ask a good question today?"**

Can cats Swim

even if they don't like water?

Answer us this:

Did Devon Rex, **Pawlympic** champion in both the 200 and 400 **meowter** races, *not* win eight gold medals? Of course cats can swim! She was a champion because her webbed toes—which all cats have—helped her zoom through water with **purrrfect** form. Tigers love to swim. Domestic cats can swim too, but most simply prefer to stay dry.

Why do squirrels **stare** and scamper away?

8

They stare because you fascinate them.

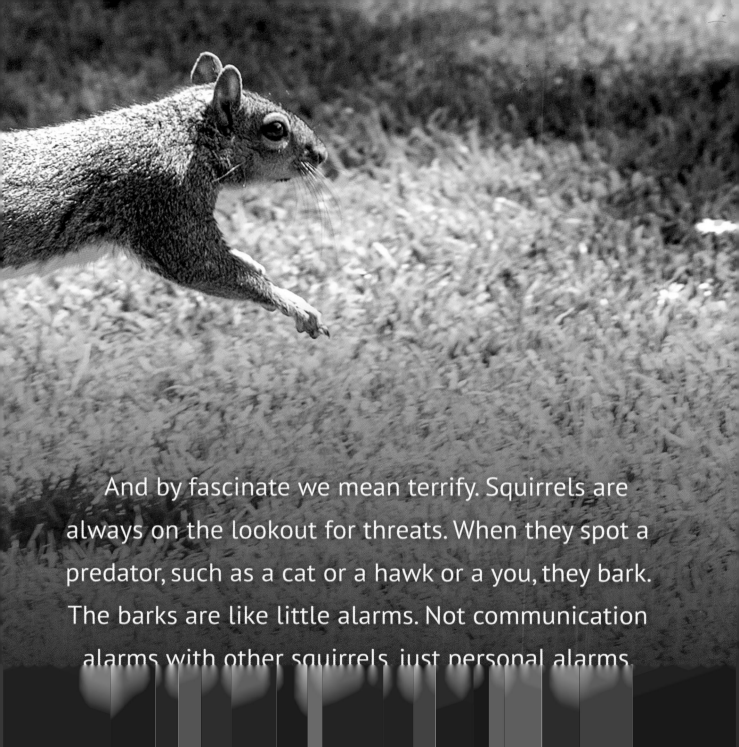

And by fascinate we mean terrify. Squirrels are always on the lookout for threats. When they spot a predator, such as a cat or a hawk or a you, they bark. The barks are like little alarms. Not communication alarms with other squirrels, just personal alarms.

Do porcupines launch their quills?

No, porcupines can't shoot quills at their enemies.

But wouldn't that be awesome? "Pow, take that!" Porcupines aren't that aggressive. When disturbed, they will raise and shake their quills and stamp their feet as a warning. When they're attacked, they strike enemies with their quilled tails. The quills come out easily and stick into the attacker's flesh. Then they grow new quills to replace those they lost.

How does catnip affect cats

and make them all loony?

Catnip affects cats a lot like your favorite food affects you. The food makes you so happy that you want to eat it forever and ever. A cat exposed to catnip might rub its head and body on the herb, roll around in it, chew it, meow, and generally act crazier than usual. Just as your favorite food might also be your parents' favorite food, cats inherit their love of catnip. So not all cats are affected. For those that are, the effect lasts about 10 minutes. Then the cat starts acting normal again.

Do hamsters ever throw up after all that spinning?

Thankfully, we haven't had to do too many vomit cleanups.

But it wouldn't be surprising. Hamsters store great amounts of food in their fat cheeks. And hamsters can run more than five miles in one evening. So...a long run mixed with a lot of food may not end well. Running on a wheel is great exercise for a hamster. It helps your hamster stay fit.

Do pigs dance?

Only if they really like the song!

How can birds fly?

29

They believe in themselves!

That, and their anatomy helps, too. A bird's wing is curved on top and flat or slightly curved on the bottom. When air whirls around the wing, it flows faster over the top part than the bottom part. The flow of air creates an upward force called *lift.* That enables birds to rise and flap, flap, flap through the sky.

Why do dogs smell each other's behinds?

33

For a dog, sniffing a behind is like learning the name and face of a new friend. They use scent for communication. Dogs have a pair of glands at their rear end. These glands produce an odor. When one dog meets another, that dog may get up close and have a good sniff. This way, they will recognize their new friend next time they meet. Want to try this with someone you meet? Don't! Our sense of smell isn't nearly as well-developed as a dog's. You'll have to stick with a boring handshake.

Why are beavers so dang adorable?

We can't exactly explain the science behind beavers being so adorable,

but here are some beaver facts, so you can decide. Thousands of years ago, some North American beavers grew to be about 7 ½ feet (2.3 meters) long—nearly as big as grizzly bears. Beavers have three eyelids on each eye. We at World Book think they're so dang adorable because of their colossal chompers.

Do frogs see in the dark?

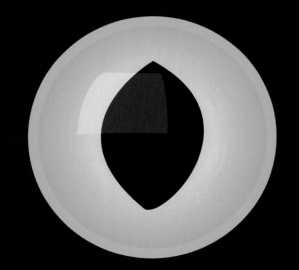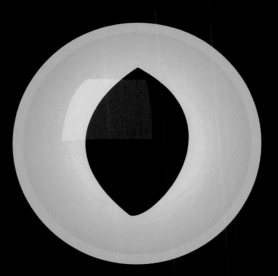

41

Is that what you've been toad?

Frogs *can* see in the dark. Frogs and toads have better night vision than many other animals—humans included. Now that you've learned this information, we hope you don't **frog**-et.

Why do horses smile?

Because they are happy to see you.

Horses can both read human facial expressions and remember them. So, if you were cheerful around a horse that morning, it would be cheerful around you in the afternoon. Smiling is only one of horses' 17 facial expressions. For instance, they can make puppy-dog eyes to show fear.

Are wolves related to dogs?

Yes!

Dogs are the domesticated descendants of wolves. To domesticate means to adapt something for human use. From domestication comes many breeds, or kinds of dogs. Poodle, Labrador retriever, and Siberian husky are examples of breeds. Dogs and wolves are still so closely related that dogs are considered a subspecies of the wolf species.

How high
can frogs jump,
and why do
they ribbit?

Some frogs have short hind legs,

which means they can't leap far. But many frogs can leap 20 times their body length. That's a lot of spring in their step! As for the ribbiting: frogs are

a lot like boy bands. In most frog species, only males call. When you hear a frog sound, it's a male frog looking for a mate. So, they make noises to look for love. See how they're like boy bands?

Can pets learn to say words? If so, how?

57

If you ask a dog, "What do you call the outer covering of a tree?" she might reply, "Bark!" But all jokes aside, dogs can't speak words from human language. But do you know what pet can? Parrots. They can mimic what you say, but they may not fully understand what the words mean. Parrots learn by listening. They listen to the sounds and imitate them.

Feed me!

Why are cows so fat?

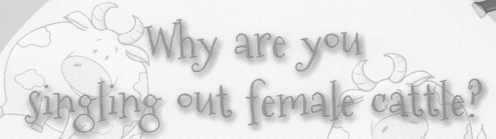

Why are you singling out female cattle?

Cow refers only to female cattle. Both male and female cattle aren't fat, anyway. They are muscular. That seems right, because their product (milk) makes *you* muscular. Cattle do have pretty big bodies, though, and they need a lot of food to fuel them. They store that food in a stomach that has *four* chambers!

63

Why do dogs pant?

To cover their rear ends.

Oh, sorry. We thought you asked, "Why do dogs wear **pants**?" But, *if a dog wore pants,* it would start to pant. When dogs get too hot—like, if they wear pants—they pant to cool off. Panting moves air through a dog's body to cool her down. Dogs pant for other reasons, too. They may be excited or, unfortunately, ill. Be sure to learn your dog's behavior, so you can be the best patroller of puppy panting the dog world has ever seen!

Do sheep get cold when you shave their wool?

69

Yes!

The thick wool of sheep is meant to keep the animals warm. But, their thick wool also puts them at risk of overheating. So, sheep ranchers usually shear their sheep in the spring. That's when the weather is warm, but before it gets too hot in the summer. They don't want their sheep to feel too **baa-d**.

How do reptiles shed their skin?

They dance and wriggle around.

We'll explain this process with one of the most rhythmic animals: a snake. New scales form under the old layer of scales. The skin on the snout gets loose first. Then the snake pushes and shimmies and shakes the skin backwards against a rock or the stem of a plant. The snake then crawls out of the old skin and sheds it in one piece. Then it holds for applause.

Will touching a toad give me warts?

No way!

We bet a toad who didn't want *your* germs told you that. Toads usually have rough, bumpy skin. Glands within the skin form raised areas that look like warts. But they're not. However, since these raised areas resemble warts, there are superstitions that a person can get warts from touching a toad. No need to worry—be **hoppy** this isn't true!

Why do bees hug?

To stay warm.

And because they are so sweet—sweet like honey. Bees huddle together in the winter, because they do not hibernate and need to keep warm. The bees keep warm by shivering and crowding together. This crowding helps to seal off escaping heat. And the shivering helps make heat. If the bees keep shivering, the temperature of the hive can reach over 90 °F (over 32 °C).

Why do glowworms glow?

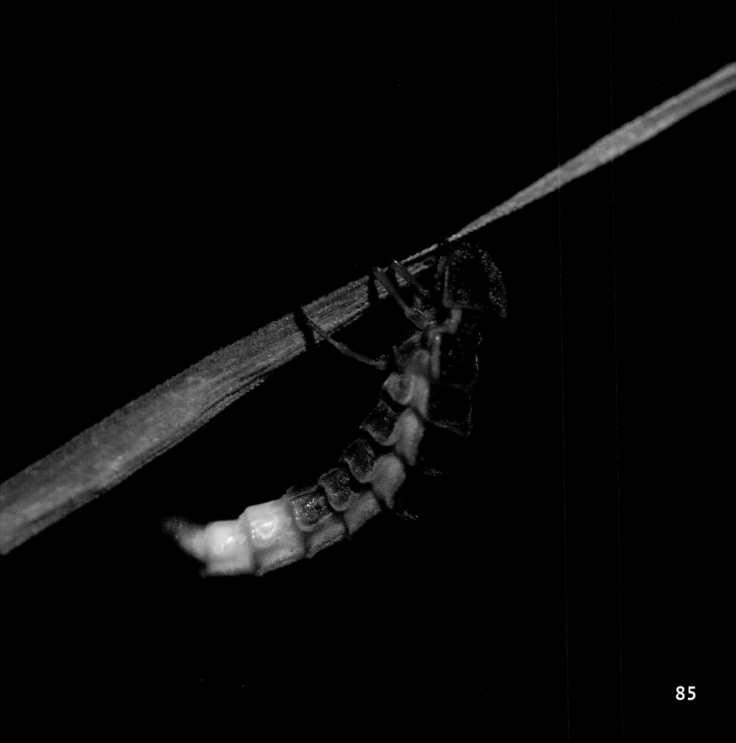

They moisturize.

And they have tiny flashlights inside. Glowworms glow a beautiful blue-green color because of a chemical process called bioluminescence. The glow starts at the rear of the insect. Then a reflective organ radiates the glow. When a bunch of glowworms get together, they make striking displays. They look like a galaxy of stars!

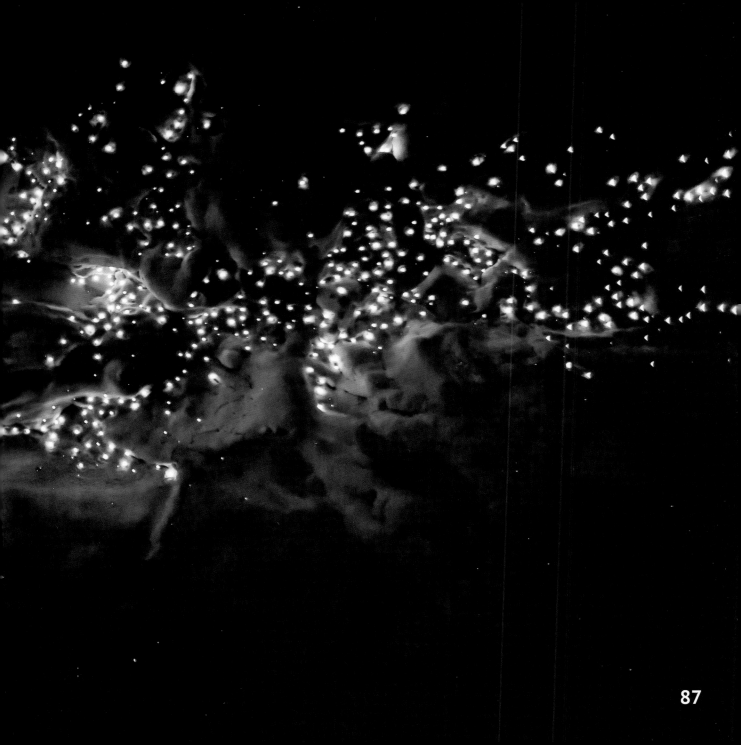

How do flies communicate?

Flies don't need to communicate with each other very much.

But, if they did, it would need to be **on the fly,** because they are constantly zipping and zooming to avoid annoyed humans. The buzzing sound from a fly—and helping the annoyed human find the pest—isn't used for communication. When they need to communicate, they use their complex eyes and strong senses of smell.

How long can a rabbit's teeth get?

A rabbit's teeth could be 75 inches (191 centimeters) long. Pet rabbits live about 10 to 15 years, but wild rabbits only live about 6 years. A rabbit's teeth grow 3 to 5 inches (8 to 13 centimeters) each year. But a rabbit's teeth could never actually be 75 inches long, because they grind their food to wear down the ever-growing teeth. With teeth that long, there's no way a rabbit could dance to its favorite music: **hip-hop.**

World Book, Inc.
180 North LaSalle Street
Suite 900
Chicago, Illinois 60601
USA

For information about other "Answer Me This, World Book" titles, as well as other World Book print and digital publications, please go to www.worldbook.com.

For information about other World Book publications, call 1-800-WORLDBK (967-5325).

For information about sales to schools and libraries, call 1-800-975-3250 (United States) or 1-800-837-5365 (Canada).

Library of Congress Cataloging-in-Publication Data for this volume has been applied for.

Answer Me This, World Book
ISBN: 978-0-7166-3821-6 (set, hc.)

Can cats swim even if they don't like water?
World Book answers your questions about pets and other animals
ISBN: 978-0-7166-3825-4 (hc.)

Also available as:
ISBN: 978-0-7166-3835-3 (e-book)

Printed in China by RR Donnelley,
Guangdong Province
1st printing July 2019

Acknowledgments

Cover © Akugasahagy/Shutterstock; © Selin Serhii, Shutterstock;
       © Ermolaev Alexander, Shutterstock
3-95   © Shutterstock

Staff

Editorial

Writers
Madeline King
Grace Guibert

Manager, New Content Development
Jeff De La Rosa

Manager, New Product Development
Nick Kilzer

Proofreader
Nathalie Strassheim

Manager, Contracts and Compliance
(Rights and Permissions)
Loranne K. Shields

Manager, Indexing Services
David Pofelski

Digital

Director, Digital Product
Development
Erika Meller

Digital Product Manager
Jonathan Wills

Graphics and Design

Senior Visual
Communications Designer
Melanie Bender

Media Editor
Rosalia Bledsoe

Manufacturing/Production

Manufacturing Manager
Anne Fritzinger

Production Specialist
Curley Hunter